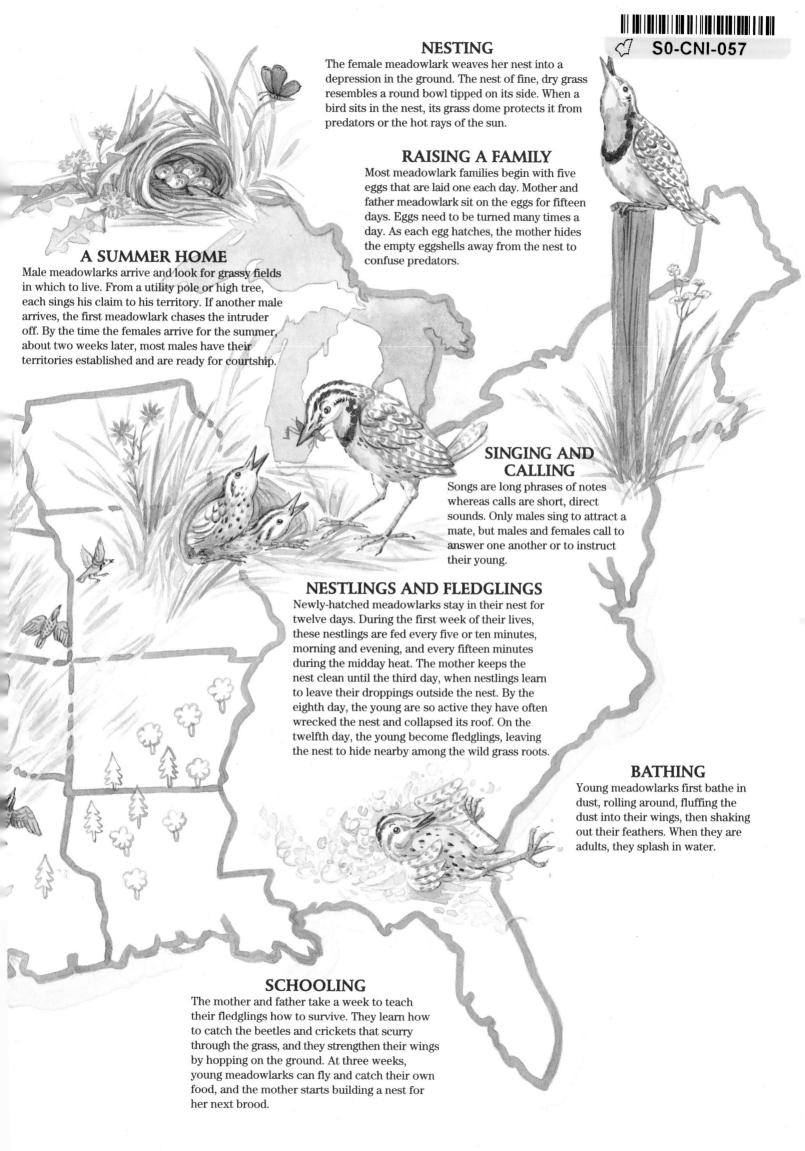

NESTING

The female meadowlark weaves her nest into a depression in the ground. The nest of fine, dry grass resembles a round bowl tipped on its side. When a bird sits in the nest, its grass dome protects it from predators or the hot rays of the sun.

RAISING A FAMILY

Most meadowlark families begin with five eggs that are laid one each day. Mother and father meadowlark sit on the eggs for fifteen days. Eggs need to be turned many times a day. As each egg hatches, the mother hides the empty eggshells away from the nest to confuse predators.

A SUMMER HOME

Male meadowlarks arrive and look for grassy fields in which to live. From a utility pole or high tree, each sings his claim to his territory. If another male arrives, the first meadowlark chases the intruder off. By the time the females arrive for the summer, about two weeks later, most males have their territories established and are ready for courtship.

SINGING AND CALLING

Songs are long phrases of notes whereas calls are short, direct sounds. Only males sing to attract a mate, but males and females call to answer one another or to instruct their young.

NESTLINGS AND FLEDGLINGS

Newly-hatched meadowlarks stay in their nest for twelve days. During the first week of their lives, these nestlings are fed every five or ten minutes, morning and evening, and every fifteen minutes during the midday heat. The mother keeps the nest clean until the third day, when nestlings learn to leave their droppings outside the nest. By the eighth day, the young are so active they have often wrecked the nest and collapsed its roof. On the twelfth day, the young become fledglings, leaving the nest to hide nearby among the wild grass roots.

BATHING

Young meadowlarks first bathe in dust, rolling around, fluffing the dust into their wings, then shaking out their feathers. When they are adults, they splash in water.

SCHOOLING

The mother and father take a week to teach their fledglings how to survive. They learn how to catch the beetles and crickets that scurry through the grass, and they strengthen their wings by hopping on the ground. At three weeks, young meadowlarks can fly and catch their own food, and the mother starts building a nest for her next brood.

KIKI
and the
CUCKOO

Written by **Elizabeth Happy**

Illustrated by **Andra Chase**

MarshMedia, Kansas City, Missouri

To George

Special thanks to
Dr. Richard Prum, Curator,
Museum of Natural History,
University of Kansas

Text © 1992 by Marsh Film Enterprises, Inc.
Illustrations © 1992 by Marsh Film Enterprises, Inc.

Published by **MARSH**media
A Division of Marsh Film Enterprises, Inc.
P. O. Box 8082
Shawnee Mission, KS 66208

Library of Congress Cataloging-in-Publication Data
Happy, Elizabeth.
   Kiki and the cuckoo/written by Elizabeth Happy; illustrated by Andra Chase.
        p. cm.
   Summary: Kiki, a western meadowlark, migrates from Texas to the Kansas prairie to make his summer home, find a wife, and have a family.
     ISBN 1-55942-038-3
     1. Meadowlarks — Juvenile fiction. [1.Meadowlarks — Fiction. 2. Birds — Fiction.] I. Chase, Andra, ill. II. Title.
PZ10.3.H226Ki   1992
[Fic]—dc20   92-27673

Book layout by Christine Nolt

Printed in Hong Kong

You would think that if Kiki the Meadowlark could find his way from Texas to Kansas, he would know enough not to pick a fight with a clock. But how clear are your thoughts when you get jealous?

One spring morning, as Kiki was flying north to find a summer home, he spotted a wide meadow laid out below him like a welcome mat. Beside it sat a farmhouse surrounded by fields of green and brown like the squares of a giant prairie quilt. The green squares sprouted winter wheat, and the brown squares were stitched into neatly plowed rows of earth.

"Nice place to live," thought Kiki, landing on a cottonwood tree. He was ready for summer, and he knew just what he must do.

"I will claim this meadow,

      I will sing beautifully, and

            I will attract a wife," he said to himself.

Kiki fanned his tail and began practicing his song. "I'm Kiki the Meadowlark, and this is my meadow," he called. Then he did a series of trills and sang "Wife! Wife! Wife!" He was about to sing about his strong wings and the wild grass seeds he was good at finding, when another voice rang out.

"I'm Pekeat the Meadowlark, and this is MY meadow!" Kiki's feathers stood up in angry tufts.

"Wife! Wife! Wife!" called the new voice.

Kiki was in the air and after the intruder in a flash. "This is MY meadow," he called. "Only I sing here!" Kiki soared high over Pekeat, then dropped toward him like a stone.

"ALL RIGHT! ALL RIGHT!" called Pekeat. "I'm going!" And he zigzagged through the trees and disappeared into the bright Kansas sky.

"Bravo," came a voice over Kiki's wing. It was Robin, landing beside Kiki. Robin was holding a little twig with his foot.

"If he sings in my meadow," explained Kiki, " a lovely meadowlark might choose him for her husband instead of me." Kiki eyed Robin suspiciously. "Do you live around here?"

"That's my place over there," said Robin, pointing his bill toward a crabapple tree at the edge of the garden. "And you don't need to worry about me. I already have a wife." In the fork of the crabapple Kiki could see a female robin working on a nest. "We're lining the walls with mud," Robin added proudly and flew off with his twig.

Kiki returned to the cottonwood and began his song again. "I'm Kiki the Meadowlark! Wife! Wife! Wife! I'm Kiki the . . . "

"Listen! Listen! Listen!" rang out, and Kiki was interrupted again.

"I'm Cuckoo! Best! Best! Best!" the new caller insisted, and by this time Kiki was ricocheting around the meadow like a balloon releasing air.

"Where is he?" fumed Kiki flying through the farmer's fields trying to get closer to the sound. But it was gone.

Kiki sat on the roof of the farmhouse. He waited and listened, waited and listened. And just when he thought maybe his new rival was gone . . .

"Cuckoo! Cuckoo! Best! Best! Best!"

Kiki dropped to the low branches of a dogwood tree, and through a window he saw the bird flapping his wings and singing. Strange nest, thought Kiki. "Listen! Listen! Listen!" he called. "I am Kiki! You can't sing here!"

"Pay no attention," said Robin. He was holding a clump of grass this time. "You'll get used to him."

"But I don't want to get used to him!" cried Kiki, jumping up and down on the branch. "That bird can't sing in MY meadow!"

"But he never goes near your meadow," observed Robin. "He never goes anywhere."

"His voice does," objected Kiki. "He's got to stop!"

"Well, he won't," said Robin.

Dejected, Kiki returned to the meadow. "I'm ruined!" he wailed. "I'll NEVER get a wife, I'll NEVER have a family, and . . . I'll be unhappy FOREVER!" He decided to sulk. Not once through the long afternoon did Kiki sing out his name or call "Wife! Wife! Wife!" And every hour, like clockwork, that strange bird's voice cut through his meadow. "Cuckoo! Cuckoo! Cuckoo! I'm best, best, best!"

The next morning, a man and a woman stood in the farmhouse flower beds washing windows. Kiki sat in the dogwood and watched. The windows of the big room where the cuckoo lived were raised high.

Suddenly the little door to the cuckoo's house flew open and out he popped. "Listen! Listen! Listen!" he called. Instantly Kiki was in the air, through the open window, and diving straight for the cuckoo.

17

The cuckoo never flinched. Even as Kiki bore down upon him, the bird called, "Cuckoo! Cuckoo! Cuckoo!" Even as Kiki crashed into his hard little flapping wings, he called out, "I'm best, best, best!" And then the cuckoo was dragging Kiki with him, back through the little front door. When it slammed shut, there was Kiki — his head wedged into a dark box, his wings outside, pinned by the door. Kiki's heart jumped up and down as he gulped for air. "Help! Help!" he screamed, and then "Warning! Warning!" to other birds that might be nearby.

Suddenly the small door opened and someone was pulling Kiki gently out of the box. A woman said, "How did a bird get caught in our cuckoo clock?" A girl stood beside her. "It's a meadowlark," the woman said, holding Kiki in her gloved hand.

"Let me see," whispered the girl. "Oh," she sighed, "are they all as pretty?"

"No," thought Kiki.

"Yes," said the mother. "Maybe this is the one we heard singing in the meadow."

"Mr. Meadowlark," said the girl, "you have a lovely song. Please keep singing for us." They took Kiki outside and gently tossed him into the air. The wind filled his feathers and he flew to the nearest tree. There he sat, still frightened, for a long while.

Then, from the open window, the cuckoo called to him again, "I'm best! I'm best!" And Kiki wondered if it might not be true. His heart felt as if it were being squeezed in the cuckoo's door again.

If only Kiki had listened to the girl. He might have forgotten about that silly wooden cuckoo and sung his own meadowlark song. But he didn't.

Instead Kiki decided to sing a new song, the song of his rival. "Maybe I can't get rid of that cuckoo," he told Robin, "but I'll outsing him if it's the last thing I do!" Robin just shook his head.

Kiki's new song rang across the meadow. "Listen! Listen! Listen!" he called. "I'm Kiki, the best!" But no wife came.

Finally, one afternoon, a female floated onto the meadow grass beneath Kiki's tree. Kiki threw out his chest.

"I'm best!

    I'm best!

        I'm best," he called. And watched as the meadowlark flew away. "What's wrong with my song?" he wondered. "COME BACK!" he called. "I'm a wonderful husband!"

"You are a sorry cuckoo," she twittered, then soared into the sky.

"She's right you know," came Robin's voice. "You make a wonderful meadowlark, but a bad cuckoo."

Suddenly Kiki felt very foolish. He gazed across his meadow at the grass growing taller each day. He felt the sun on his wings, warmer than yesterday. Springtime was hurrying on, but what had happened to his plan? Right then Kiki made a decision.

Arching his body, Kiki threw out his chest until his beak pointed straight up in a long, elegant line.

"Meadowlark! Meadowlark! Meadowlark!" he sang, and trilled the "meadow" and warbled the "lark" until his notes expanded like petals in the sun. "Wife! Wife! Wife!" he caroled.

"Bravo!" cried Robin.

When afternoon arrived, a lovely meadowlark landed on Kiki's branch.
"Hello," she chirped. "I'm looking for a husband that sings as well as you."

Spring grew into summer. The farmer's fields were a glossy green with the leaves of corn, milo, and soy beans. Kiki sang all day to his wife while she wove meadow grasses into a snug little domed nest. It sat on the ground, and you could hardly spot it, even if you walked close by.

And then, one summer night, when all the world was quiet, Kiki heard "Listen! Listen! Listen!" seeping out of the farmhouse and drifting across the meadow. He left his nest and sitting in the cottonwood began singing a duet with that cuckoo.

"I'm best!" called the cuckoo.

"I'm Kiki!" called the meadowlark.

"I'm best!"

"I'm Kiki!"

"I'm best!"

"I'm Kiki!"

Then the cuckoo stopped, and the little door slammed faintly in the night.

Kiki kept right on singing.

Dear Parents and Educators:

There is much debate about the value of competition for children. Some parents and educators believe that competition teaches children discipline and good sportsmanship and that it motivates them to their highest levels of performance. These parents and educators devise opportunities for children to compete formally — for a blue ribbon, a part in the school play, a spelling bee championship, a place on the soccer team.

Others argue that competition does more harm than good, that it buoys the self-esteem of a few children while it undermines the confidence of many. Some schools have, consequently, done away with score keeping and contests, and in some cases, even grades.

All agree, however, that competition in one form or another is a fact of life. By providing an example of competition to which children can relate, *Kiki and the Cuckoo* can help children cope with the competition they will inevitably encounter. Through Kiki's ordeal, they will see how quickly competition may cause us to lose sight of our personal values and goals as well as our sense of self-worth.

To help youngsters better understand the message of *Kiki and the Cuckoo,* discuss the following questions with them:

- What three things does Kiki set out to accomplish when he arrives in Kansas?

- Why does Kiki chase Pekeat out of the meadow?

- Why do you think Kiki is jealous of the cuckoo?

- Why does Kiki try to sing like the cuckoo? Have you ever tried to be like or act like someone else?

- Can you remember a time when you won in a competition? When you lost? How did you feel each time?

Here are some ways to help children cope with competition:

- Help boys and girls discover and develop their own special talents and interests.

- Point out that the strengths of others do not detract from their own strengths.

- Minimize comparisons between children.

- Encourage children to compete with themselves rather than with others.

- Provide opportunities for children to make things happen together, each contributing his or her unique abilities.

Available from MarshMedia

STORYBOOKS, VIDEOS AND ACTIVITY BOOKS

Clarissa, written by Carol Talley, illustrated by Itoko Maeno. Hardcover with dust jacket, 32 pages with full-color illustrations throughout. (MarshMedia) ISBN 1-55942-014-6. $16.95.

Clarissa video, based on the book written by Carol Talley and illustrated by Itoko Maeno. 13:00 run time. (MarshMedia) ISBN 1-55942-023-5. $59.95.

Hana's Year, written by Carol Talley, illustrated by Itoko Maeno. Hardcover with dust jacket, 32 pages with full-color illustrations throughout. (MarshMedia) ISBN 1-55942-034-0. $16.95.

Hana's Year video, based on the book written by Carol Talley and illustrated by Itoko Maeno. 17:00 run time. (MarshMedia) ISBN 1-55942-035-9. $59.95.

Kiki and the Cuckoo, written by Elizabeth Happy, illustrated by Andra Chase. Hardcover with dust jacket, 32 pages with full-color illustrations throughout. (MarshMedia) ISBN 1-55942-038-3. $16.95.

Kiki and the Cuckoo video, based on the book written by Elizabeth Happy and illustrated by Andra Chase. 13:00 run time. (MarshMedia) ISBN 1-55942-039-1. $59.95.

Kylie's Song, written by Patty Sheehan, illustrated by Itoko Maeno. Hardcover with dust jacket, 32 pages with full-color illustrations throughout. (Advocacy Press) ISBN 0-911655-19-0. $16.95.

Kylie's Song video, based on the book written by Patty Sheehan and illustrated by Itoko Maeno. 12:00 run time. (MarshMedia) ISBN 1-55942-021-9. $59.95.

Minou, written by Mindy Bingham, illustrated by Itoko Maeno. Hardcover with dust jacket, 64 pages with full-color illustrations throughout. (Advocacy Press) ISBN 0-911655-36-0. $16.95.

Minou video, based on the book written by Mindy Bingham and illustrated by Itoko Maeno. 18:30 run time. (MarshMedia) ISBN 1-55942-015-4. $59.95.

My Way Sally, written by Mindy Bingham and Penelope Paine, illustrated by Itoko Maeno. Hardcover with dust jacket, 48 pages with full-color illustrations throughout. (Advocacy Press) ISBN 0-911655-27-1. $16.95.

My Way Sally video, based on the book written by Mindy Bingham and Penelope Paine and illustrated by Itoko Maeno. 19:30 run time. (MarshMedia) ISBN 1-55942-017-0. $59.95.

Papa Piccolo, written by Carol Talley, illustrated by Itoko Maeno. Hardcover with dust jacket, 32 pages with full-color illustrations throughout. (MarshMedia) ISBN 1-55942-028-6. $16.95.

Papa Piccolo video, based on the book written by Carol Talley and illustrated by Itoko Maeno. 18:00 run time. (MarshMedia) ISBN 1-55942-029-4. $59.95.

Time for Horatio, written by Penelope Paine, illustrated by Itoko Maeno. Hardcover with dust jacket, 48 pages with full-color illustrations throughout. (Advocacy Press) ISBN 0-911655-33-6. $16.95.

Time for Horatio video, based on the book written by Penelope Paine and illustrated by Itoko Maeno. 19:00 run time. (MarshMedia) ISBN 1-55942-026-X. $59.95.

Tonia the Tree, written by Sandy Stryker, illustrated by Itoko Maeno. Hardcover with dust jacket, 32 pages with full-color illustrations throughout. (Advocacy Press) ISBN 0-911655-16-6. $16.95.

Tonia the Tree video, based on the book written by Sandy Stryker and illustrated by Itoko Maeno. 12:10 run time. (MarshMedia) ISBN 1-55942-019-7. $59.95.

An activity book full of games, puzzles, maps, and project ideas is available for each of these titles. Softcover. $14.95 each.

You can find storybooks at better bookstores. Or you may order storybooks, videos, and activity books direct by sending a check for the amount shown plus $2.50 per item for shipping to MarshMedia, P. O. Box 8082, Shawnee Mission, Kansas 66208, or by calling 1-800-821-3303.

MarshMedia has been publishing high-quality, award-winning learning materials for children since 1969. To receive a free catalog, call 1-800-821-3303.

A TYPICAL YEAR

Meadowlarks are born in the summer. By September and October, most meadowlarks—young and old—flock together to fly south and avoid winter. In February and March, they return for the summer to the states in which they were born. Meadowlarks will raise two sets of families before the chilly fall nights send them south again.

A CHOICE

The Eastern meadowlark lives from Maine to Florida, and the Western meadowlark lives from Oregon to the northern tip of Mexico. In the Midwest their territories overlap. The Western meadowlark is the state bird of Kansas. Kiki is a Western meadowlark. The Eastern and Western meadowlarks look very similar, but their songs are completely different. The Eastern meadowlark whistles a song of high, short notes. The Western meadowlark sings a greater range of lower notes that bubble into flutelike trills.

LEARNING TO SING

When he arrives in the spring, a young meadowlark male instinctively knows a basic pattern of notes. But he learns more notes by listening to other birds sing. Females are often attracted to a male with a complex song.

DANGERS

Meadowlarks avoid predators from sky and ground by hiding themselves and their nests well into the grass. Eagles, falcons, and hawks swoop from the sky, while skunks, raccoons, coyotes, and snakes attack from the ground. Threshing machines, cutting the meadow for hay, can also destroy nests. Usually, though, the second brood has left home by harvesttime.

HIDING

Although it is easy to spot a meadowlark proudly thrusting out its gold chest, a meadowlark crouching in the grass is more difficult to see. The meadowlark's speckled brown back feathers mirror the mottled patterns of grass and shadow that play across a prairie field.

TRAVELING

Meadowlarks fly at night. This may be because they have better coverage from their predators in the dark or because they can catch more insects if they eat and rest during the day.